Finished writing

I feel pink today - by Ruth kaputa.

Dear reader

Once there was a baby girl her parent's named her Ruth the first year of her life in the hospital, she called her home. The doctor's sat her parent's down and told them that their baby girl that they had been praying for had only 24 hours to live, due to liver and kidney failure. And even if the baby girl lives then what's the point of looking after and raising a vegetable who couldn't. So, the baby girl's parents prayed and had faith, and that baby girl fought hard for her life. Then she proved every doctor that ever said no to her second chance in life wrong (and she wasn't a vegetable). If you asked then 3-year-old ruth to sum up her life in a few words she would probably say "a lot of hospital, nursery and CBeebies and Peppa pig, speech and language therapy and physiotherapy. The doctors said she will have to go through it for the rest of her life, but when she was 12 years old her speech and language therapist, ruth worked hard and proved all those doctors wrong again the speech and language therapist said that she didn't need speech and language therapy anymore and she's working hard stop physiotherapy for ever. You see all her life she had been proving people wrong, but it was time to prove herself wrong. When ruth decided to be a writer she wanted to write a book, but her subconscious told her otherwise, "you have to be an adult to write and publish a book" but she did her research and learnt that there is NO LIMIT to her dream. So, at the ripe old age of 13 she wrote a book called I feel pink today after her favourite colour PINK anyway this is a bit about the book you're reading.

This is the story of your author (AKA me) Ruth kaputa.

WARNING BEFORE YOU READ THIS BOOK:

Dumb jokes discased as song refences. The author ruth kaputa (ME) is quite a chatter box in the words of my mum. So, if you don't like that YOU CAN LEAVE **(by that I mean close the book and return it) (I was joking please keep reading)**

Season 1- get to know me, (Ruth Kaputa!)

Hi, my name is Ruth kaputa I am currently 13 years old; I'm from London but my mum is from Sierra Leon and my personal assistant I mean dad is from Congo *(my dad is from the south and my mum is from the west of Africa)* and I have 2 brothers one is older Akeem and one younger Nehemiah (but we call him Nehe for short it's nah like a horse). and I love PINK *(not the artist the colour love)* *(although I do like the song "I wanna start a fight")*. My favourite movie is sister act 2 *(back in the habit)* you should really watch it but watch the first sister act to understand the storyline. My favourite actresses are Whoopie Goldberg, Naomi Ackie, Brandy Norwood, and Jennifer Hudson *(if you don't know them you can google them)*. I'm a big music lover. I love glee covers and 90s R&B and pop music like Whitney Houston, Stevie Wonder, Megan Trainor, Adele *(she's not 90s but still)*, and Brandy Norwood and my favourite bands are glee covers, boy 2 men and the cheetah girls. Before I start, I am so sorry If I waffle a lot and the dumb jokes *(wow I talk a lot)*. In this book instead of chapters *(because that sounds boring)* it's going to have seasons like a tv show and instead of me being the author I'm the writer/ executive producer/director. I'm a writer and when I grow up, I want to write storylines for movies and tv shows oh and soaps like neighbours and home and away *(there Australian soaps) (I'm a huge fan of both)*. In this short book we shall talk about different topics from society and Hollywood to self-love and self-esteem, motivation. I have left side cerebral palsy if you don't know what that is then JUST GOOGLE IT *(just joking)* cerebral palsy is a scar in the brain that weakens my muscles on the left side of my body. That's why I use my right hand a lot and I mean a lot in fact as I type this my left arm is a lazy couch potato just sitting there. My wish is as you read this you will treat and see me as a normal person because I am. When I tell people to not call me disabled, they called me differently abled, and I say no because I see myself as normal, I just have challenges that affect my daily life but don't we all. I feel like there must be trust in our relationship between the writer/ executive producer/director and the viewer, so the truth is *(ha-ha see what I did there ruth and truth, no okay)* anyway I'm a three-time published poet I'm telling the truth *(Opps I did it again) (Britney spears)*. in this short book I want teach you how to treat people like me feel normal but anyway, have stories that will make you cry so hard that you laugh and laugh so hard that you cry. I was born on the 1st of April 2010 *(I know 2010 worst year because the spice girls and one direction broke up, I know it was hard, but we powered though the pain)* at 11am *(nearly lunch time so that's why I like food so much) (I know April fools ha-ha)* when I was born the doctors said I had 24 hours to live they basically didn't have faith or hope in me. But *(ha-ha doctors I'm alive)* I was in a coma. So, they had to inject my brain with coffee to wake me up *(even though I don't like coffee)* in fact there's a picture of me in the coma as a baby on the next page and I'm in a wheelchair because I can't walk for long. Now we will be discussing my learning disability. A learning disability is when you don't process things at the same rate as other people, but for me I forget things I have a very good memory, but I forget things academically which affects my learning. Although there are subjects that do somehow stick in my head more than others like history or English but other subjects like maths, science just doesn't stick. It (the learning disability) makes you feel dumb because you know you should know the answers to your test, but you struggle quite a lot. So, this the end of the road *(get it boys 2 men no...ok tough crowd)* any Hoo see you in the next season.

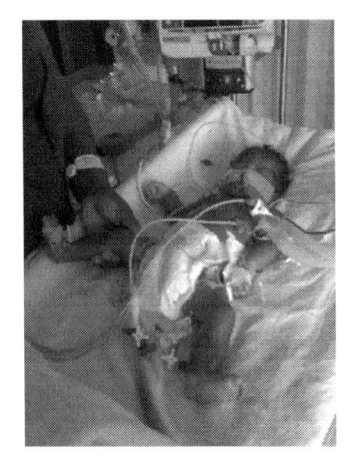

← this is me in the coma (now it looks painful, but I DIDN'T FEEL ANYTHiNG)

season 2 – my poetry

Hi as I said in season 1 I I'm a poet, so I want to show you some of my work. Let's begin!

I know everything – by Ruth Kaputa

Mummy and daddy and are fighting again this time mummy has a BIG SCRACH on her head.

Mummy and daddy are fighting again this time daddy walked out normally he comes back DRUNK but this time he didn't.

Mummy and daddy are fighting again this time mummy came to my room with TEARS DOWN HER FACE as she said "everything is going to be okay" but I knew everything wasn't okay I KNOW EVERYTHING

I know about the ABUSE and the SHARDS OF GLASS mummy picks up every single night.

Normally its mummy and daddy who are fighting its normally daddy SCREAMING at mummy and all Mummy can do is watch the man she once loved turn into An ABUSIVE MONSTER I KNOW EVERYTHING.

I know some of you cried because some of you been though it or you know someone whose been through it, I haven't been through it. I'll give you one more since you're begging.

Dear Gen Z's – by Ruth Kaputa

Dear Gen Z's I'm sorry a million trees have been cut down simply because of logging, agriculture mining and so much more.

Dear Gen Zs as a Gen Z myself I truly thank you on millennials and boomers because as you sat there and watched repeats of George Floyd being brutally murdered by police you decided to say something about it.

I also thank you for learning about how strong black men and woman joined Dr martin Luther king on the Eddison bridge in Alabama to fight for what for what they believed in, and you said it was right.

Dear Gen Z's I'm sorry that America is still called a free country after seeing single mothers choosing nappes over food.

We're not just doing silly TikTok we're doing hashtag black lives matter; we're doing hashtag help stop climate change. We're changing the world so let us. Dear Gen Zs thank you.

Here's one more poem.

Meet my friend – by Ruth Kaputa

Meet my friend p she arrived in a fancy pink limousine with diamonds in a fancy red dress. On the 27th of November 2022 at around 8:30 or 9pm. She burst into my room without knocking. She said, "hi you signed up for the lifetime membership" I said, "I didn't" she said, "every woman is forced to sign up". Only my mum is allowed to see p God forbid my dad or brothers see p we might as well call the church. Some woman sugar quote it as "it's just cramps and bleeding and a lot of chocolate" but to some woman it's a funeral for their womb, the blood Opps mean her red dress reminding them as much as she tries, she will never become a woman unless she has a pram with the sound of a baby crying inside. Meet my friend p when you get to know her you learn that she's not my friend p, she's, my PERIOD.

I hope you liked that it was meant to be a radge poem about periods and about how society views periods because in my work I tell the truth. I personally think that some writers don't tell the truth, they make fairy tales with happy ending's but sometimes that's not always the case.

Now I know this chapter is about my poetry and I know in chapter two I spoke about life and potential. But I would like to share my little theory about life. Do you know how people say that "life is like a roller coaster; it goes up and down" well I think life is abstract. For example, Pablo Picasso one of the greatest artists of all time, when he started his art people thought it was strange but after people realised it was an artistic masterpiece. My point is sometimes life is abstract, going all over the place. but at the end of the day people will realise your life was an artistic masterpiece. I guess that's the end of this season I really hope you enjoyed bye.

season 3- Let me motivate you!

In this season I want to tell you that you can do anything and everybody has potential you just must find it and use it because it took Thomas Edison one thousand times to invent the light bulb, but everyone remembers the one thousandth and one time which was the light bulb he never gave up so maybe it will take you a thousand times to find your potential but never give up because everyone might just remember the a thousandth and first. I have learnt that life is like a house you can kick people out or keep them in. Because you may have negative people that push you down in your life that you need to get rid of and there will be positive people that will push you up. You need to keep the people that are positive. And remember YOU CAN DO ANYTHING YOU SET YOUR HEART AND MIND TOO because you know what they say, "A dream is a wish your heart makes" *(ok maybe it was snow white but it's true)*. Potential can also be what you want to be when you grow up. My journey finding my potential was quite a long road to cross because when I was little, I wanted to be a doctor because I wanted to help people. But then I realized I don't want to work with puck or vomit or pee or poo, but I don't mind blood, oh and medical school is too long, and I believe there's more to life than school *(but school is important)*. Then I wanted to be a pop or gospel singer, but I sound like a frog. Then an actress but I don't have patience for all the rehearsals. And then in year 7 we started doing music tech I liked it, so I wanted to be a music technician but then I realized it was just a hobby. And then I discovered my love for writing through a poetry competition which I won at my school. And here I am a three-time published poet and an author *(well when this gets published)*. So, as you can see from my journey, I had potential it just took me a long time to find my potential. I found it eventually, its ok to take long we are all human. It's okay to make mistakes. I make mistakes, you make mistakes, your mum makes mistakes even your loving grandmother who makes the best cookies make mistakes. And I didn't name it that for no reason so in the table below I will tell you the positives and negatives of why it sucks having a disability, and unfortunately there are more lows than highs, *(in a table)*. Let's begin!

Positives	Negatives
• I can eat in class	• Muscle pain
• I get a one-to-one TA which is a teaching assistant but TAs sound cooler (I call them a personal bestie)	• A lot of medication (which taste bad)
• I get to go five minutes early from class.	• People on the street steer at me for being in a wheelchair.
• Proving people wrong when they talk to you like a baby.	• People look at me with pity without getting to know me or my story.
	• People assuming you can't walk just because you're in a wheelchair.

Now we've been though that your probably confused. On why I can eat in class, you see I have hypoglycaemia which means sometimes the glucose *(sugar)* in my body runs out and if I don't get injected with an injection it has to be in the fridge or there's the gel that I keep that tastes like berries I will collapse or go into a seizer. And I bet your really confused on the last point. Anyway, you need a break from reading me so get your favourite chocolate or if you don't like chocolate stop reading, get out and think about what made you take this book. I was joking because I'm broke aren't we all in this British economy.

season 4 - why loosing people and change can be important.

In other seasons I've already given you advice about life and your potential but in this season, I have else in mind. Lisen, I know this may sound harsh, but its true people will leave you in life and sometimes you think they will be in your life forever, but the truth is people come and go and you think your life won't be the same without them. I had two teachers I was so attached to them, and they told me that they were leaving I was obviously sad because I imagined opening my GCSE results with them there but then I realized that it was their time to leave I also realized that they had an opportunity to better their career. The truth is the world small, they moved away but, in a way, they are around the corner or across the road. So, you have two choices ether stay sad for the rest of your life or stay in touch and be happy for that person or people. So, which one will you choose I'm hoping you choose the second chose. So that's why having to train yourself to deal with change is important in life because things might change but the thing that it changes into might be better. It's okay to cry I cried when they told me they were leaving I cried twice but now I make sure to keep in touch with them. I know this was a short and sad season but as I said before you must deal with change so see you in the next season.

Season 5 - a little more advice for LIFE!

In this season I will give more advice about life. These are the 5 things (in segment's) that we will go through in this season. Before we go through this most of it is about fear *(in billet points)* LET'S BEGIN.

- Have a big imagination in life!
- Jump on idea's you have in life.
- Don't let other people dim your light so they can shine.
- God closes a door to open another one.
- The power of words

Have a big imagination in life!

Now we shall talk about having a big imagination in life and fear limited visions. Fear limited visions are dreams and visions that you have or had that you've never worked on because of fear. It can also be that you can't see yourself being the big and successful person you hope, dream, and want to be. Les brown once said, "fear can crush dreams and kills hope", so when you are afraid you can easily give up your dreams go too. If you let fear control your dreams and hopes, there will be no dreams and hopes. So don't you dare ever let fear control your life and even if your plans don't work in life, you keep trying. For example, if you want to be an actress but your too scared to audition but you read this and you audition, but you didn't get the part you wanted so you don't let fear control you and you audition for a bigger part. So don't ever let fear control you or your life. Another reason is that people can't see themselves with that dream they wanted to accomplish or out of the situation they are in. For example, people in abusive relationships can't or struggle to see themselves without that person. So, what I'm trying to say is that you really should try to see yourself out of the situation and/or accomplishing that dream. See you in the next segment.

Jump on idea's you have in life!

In life if you have ideas that you think it's good then jump on it les brown once said when you die one day and there are three ghosts, those ghosts represent all the idea's that you had but didn't do anything about it and they are upset because the ideas could of made you very successful but you were scared because you thought you would fail in life. I also believe that if you don't take risks in life, it's not life, now I do not mean jump of a cliff in the name of taking risks I just mean jump on those ideas and even if you fail never give up. I have to admit there was a time where I myself did not practise what I have preached, you see when I was around ten or eleven years old this idea of the book came to mind, I thought to do this big project I have to be an adult because of my young age. And the idea was stuck at the back of my head for two to three years. But then I thought "FLIP

IT LIFE IS TOO SHORT to wait". So here I am at home in a pink and white striped very comfy jump suit writing a book. And yes, I do regret not jumping on the idea at the time. But I believe that everything in life happens at a certain time if you make it happen at the time. So, see you in the next segment.

Don't let other people dim your light so they can shine.

I believe that everyone carries a light. And I know we discussed potential but what some people don't know is that other can't handle that light that you carry. So that person will give you reasons to tone it down. For example, if you have the potential to sing. That person might say "you sing too loud" if that happens sing the loudest you can (without destroying your vocal cords of course). Your light belongs to everyone, it'll be illuminated because you were bold enough to let your light shine. Sometimes you walk into a room and your too scared to give 100 percent of your light. Most of the time you think people won't accept 100 percent sometimes they accept 50 or even 20 percent. But hon they only accept little of you because they can't handle your light or their triggered because your light is brighter than the brightest star in the night sky. So please Don't let other people dim your light so they can shine. See you in the next segment.

God closes a door to open another one.

Now before I start, I get that some of you don't believe in God, but this is from my life and my experience. I will tell you a story that happened to me, this story changed my life. This happened 2 or 3 years ago I was choosing where I was going for secondary, and I had my dream school in mind let's call it black coats (because I don't want to get sued). Now the reason I wanted to go to black coats because all my friends were going there and all the club I wanted. I couldn't go because the lift I needed I had to be in year 9 to get the lift. When I didn't get in, I was so sad, (I cried myself to sleep with a bar of chocolate) but I went to another school (the school I am in now) and I made friends and met people who I have truly found inner happiness with who I see every day and those people are the TAs they make my day every day. Then a year later I realized that God close that door to open another door. And I also realized even though I would have had my friends I wouldn't achieve inner happiness. See you in the next segment.

The power of words

Now I believe in the power of words. Words are powerful because they can make you and break you. We use words every single day, sometimes writers like me use big and small words to emphasise how big or how small something is. I believe that words hold more power than anything in the whole world. That's why you should be careful with what words you use every day and think before you say something. You know the phrase "sticks and stones may break your bones, but words will never hurt you", I HATE IT I even made a poem (that's how much I hate the phrase) this is the poem...

sticks and stones may break your bones, but words will never hurt you. Sticks stones breaks bones words never hurt me. You know that used to be motivation in life. But the real reason people say that is to hide the pain its causing inside. Because one, two or even three words can cause you pain. For example, "I love you" because love is like a drug, you go back to the thing that caused you pain in the first place. Love is a drug; people will use you and abuse all in the name of love but you're the one with the choice to let that person or people use you. So, if you want to lose your self-respect just to please other people go ahead and enjoy the ride because no one's stopping you. WORDS HURT!

so please be careful with your words and always use positive words in every situation good or bad, See you in the next season.

Season 6 – why I strongly dislike society.

In this season we are going to discuss why I strongly dislike society. Now in this book we keep it PG so I'm not going to say the H- word *(I think we all know what that is) …. (hate)*. So, these are the reasons I don't like society, *(in bullet points)* LETS BEGIN.

- Racism
- Sexism *(misogyny)*
- Normalising stuff
- Telling you what makes you successful.

- **Racism**

Before we start, I am going to not only target society, but I will also target the film industry and Hollywood, so if you don't like that you can skip this season (don't say I didn't warn you). Let's start with quite sensitive topic, its racism as a black person I just don't get why some people have a problem with other people having melamine. I feel like not only society, but Hollywood and the film industry makes it worse because in nearly every movie or tv show about black people in the south is about drugs, prison, gangs, murder or repainting black people as thugs or criminals. So, what people watch reflex how they treat people in reality. Hollywood and the film industry makes it so realistic, so the racist stereotypical black man thug idea on tv really reflex in the mind of Karen's *(sorry if your name Karen and your nice)*. That's why when I grow up and graduate university, I'm planning to create my own production company called Ruthie's art production. One more thing is those racist women who tell other people and I quote to "go back your country" when they forget that historically the native Americans (modern Indians) were in America first

- **sexism (misogyny)**

Anyway, let's move on to sexism (misogyny) even though we're in the twenty first century mostly men still think of women as objects. In some culture's young the age as me if not younger are still being forced to have babies with men up to double their age whilst others are forced to get marry men double their age. We still have the police who think they have power to sexualise young women to get what they want. And then another reason is us hating on other women/girls over boys because boys will be there forever, I don't get why girls lose 1 hour after school in detention fighting over one boy that's probably not even in school.

- **Normalising stuff**

Now shall discuss society and the film industry normalising stuff this also comes under black people being represented as bad people. Because the industry has normalised the black man thug idea Another thing is that Hollywood normalised in society is that "Africa is a forest" and that "Africa doesn't have water" when in reality Africa is one of the richest continents in the world. It's not just Hollywood I blame for the stereotypical racist Wakanda version of Africa, that they have built in people's mind. I blame the people that chose to believe these racist ideas without doing their research about Africa, I highly recommend you should go you will experience things you never thought you would experience; this is a message for the people think Africa is a country, how do you go through nursery, primary secondary, college and university. Some of you go and get two degrees, master's and PHDs and you still think Africa is a country. In-fact yes Africa is a country, and the capital city is Wakanda (it was a joke). before. Another thing society has normalised is the word "ugly," I believe that no one is born ugly society has just normalised the word to separate people considered less attractive from people considered more attractive, but remember you are so beautiful and never put a price tag on your worth because YOU ARE WORTH THE WORLD AND MORE.

- **Telling you what makes you successful.**

Now before we end the season, I would like to talk about how society telling you what makes you successful. I'll give you three successful people according to society (*in bullet points*).

- Michael Jackson
- Whitney Houston
- Prince

These people were considered very successful until their deaths, all of them did do drugs so they weren't really happy because the media made their lives look good when it wasn't. I believe that success is when you achieve inner happiness. So, these people achieved happiness financially, but they didn't achieve inner happiness. Researchers found out that worldwide only 15% of people are actually engaged in their jobs whilst 85% are unhappy with their jobs, so the 85% of the unhappy people may be making six or even seven figures and the 15% are making less but are still happy. I want to be a writer because when write I go to my own world in my imagination. And I want to be NO I AM THAT 15% of people who have found inner happiness. And if you're that 85% that is unhappy, I need you to take a break and think what makes you happy. Your life is your story, your imagination so you write it. You're the author and with writing you have to take risks so why don't you take risks in life, I'm not saying jump off a cliff or something I mean say you want to be an actor and you have an audition but you don't think you will get the part so you give up but then you decide to take a risk and you audition and you get the lead role, so take risks it might just change your life. So, I guess season 5 was long so see you in season 6.

Season 7 - selflove

in this season I will be teaching you how to love yourself. As people sometimes we get thoughts, thoughts that are not nice, but we are human and its ok. So, these are some positive thoughts that you should think and negative thoughts that you shouldn't think *(in a table)*.

Negative thoughts	Positive thoughts
"I am dumb"	I am so smart
"I am ugly"	My beauty fill's every room I go in
"I am weird"	I am so unique
"no one likes me"	I am so loved
"I wish I could be just like her/him"	I am and will always be myself

Every day I want you to look in the mirror and say the positive thoughts out loud, you can even make a fun poster. Something else you could do is get a picture of a younger version of you put the picture on your mirror so when you are telling yourself those negative thoughts remind yourself that you're calling that little girl or boy "ugly and stupid" *(basically all the negative thoughts)*

Why is selflove so important?

Research shows that having more self- compassion builds resilience in the face of adversity. It means when you practice self-love then you have enough confidence to overcome challenges in life. It is also important because if you don't love yourself, you don't know how to love other people. Self-respect is a fundamental part of self- love because again you will never learn to respect others.

What self-love looks like?

- Forgiving yourself when you mess up.
- Meeting your own needs
- Being assertive
- Not letting others take advantage of or abuse you.
- Prioritizing your health and wellbeing
- Spending time around people who support you and build you up (and avoiding people who don't)

- Asking for help
- Letting go of grudges or anger that holds you back.
- Recognizing your strengths
- Valuing your feelings
- Making healthy choices most of the time
- Living in accordance with your values
- Pursuing your interests and goals
- Challenging yourself
- Holding yourself accountable
- Giving yourself healthy treats
- Accepting your imperfections
- Setting realistic expectations

Some self- love quotes you can use.

Now I have gave you positive thoughts you can think and practise these are some quotes you can use and decorate your room with *(in bullet points) (whoop, whoop).*

- If you have the ability to love, love yourself first." – Charles Bukowski
- "The man who does not value himself, cannot value anything or anyone." – Ayn Rand
- "Be the love you never received." – Rune Lazuli
- "Love yourself first and everything else falls into line." – Lucille Ball
- "Talk to yourself like someone you love." – Brene Brown
- "To fall in love with yourself is the first secret to happiness." – Robert Morely
- "No one can make you feel inferior without your consent." – Eleanor Roosevelt
- "You are free, you are powerful, you are good, you are love, you have value, you have a purpose." – Unknown
- "You carry so much love in your heart. Give some to yourself." —R.Z.
- "How you love yourself is how you teach others to love you." —Rupi Kaur
- "Make yourself a priority." —Unknown

Fun facts about self- love

Now we've talked about why self -love is important, what it looks like, and we have looked at expert quotes and now we shall look at fun facts before end the seasons.

- Accepting yourself can make you happier.
- It could encourage you to reach those health goals.
- Self-compassion may help with mental health issues.

- It can push you to stop procrastinating.
- Loving yourself can lead you through adversity.
- If you don't love yourself, you will regret it later in life.

Well, I guess this shall be the end of the season, just a disclaimer season 6 and 7 both have to do with self-confidence. See you in the next season.

Season 8- Self esteem

In this season, in the topic of last season *(self- love)* we will be discussing self- esteem. So hopefully the things I told you about positive and negative thoughts and self- love worked and built up your self- esteem.

What is self- esteem?

Self-esteem is how we value and perceive ourselves. It's based on our opinions and beliefs about ourselves, which can feel difficult to change. We might also think of this as self-confidence. Its okay if your self-esteem low because we are human all that matters is that you fix it with these tips.

Your self-esteem can affect whether you:

- Like and value yourself as a person!
- Can make decisions and assert yourself.
- Recognise your strengths!
- Feel able to try new or difficult things.
- Show kindness towards yourself.
- Move past mistakes without blaming yourself unfairly.
- Take the time you need for yourself.
- Believe you matter and are good enough!
- Believe you deserve happiness!

How to improve your self esteem

- Be kind to yourself.
- Try to recognise the positives.
- Build a good support network.
- Try taking therapy.
- Set yourself a challenge.
- Look after yourself.

Now let's through why you should use these 6 reasons.

Be kind to yourself.

- **Get to know yourself.** For example, what makes you happy and what you value in life. You might find it helpful to write this in a journal.
- **Try to challenge unkind thoughts about yourself.** You might automatically put yourself down. If you find yourself doing this, it can help to ask: "Would I talk to a friend in this way?"

Started writing- 15/09/2023.

Finished writing – 30/12/2023 at 11:33am.

I feel pink today - by Ruth kaputa.

Dear reader

Once there was a baby girl her parent's named her Ruth the first year of her life in the hospital, she called her home. The doctor's sat her parent's down and told them that their baby girl that they had been praying for had only 24 hours to live, due to liver and kidney failure. And even if the baby girl lives then what's the point of looking after and raising a vegetable who couldn't. So, the baby girl's parents prayed and had faith, and that baby girl fought hard for her life. Then she proved every doctor that ever said no to her second chance in life wrong (and she wasn't a vegetable). If you asked then 3-year-old ruth to sum up her life in a few words she would probably say "a lot of hospital, nursery and CBeebies and Peppa pig, speech and language therapy and physiotherapy. The doctors said she will have to go through it for the rest of her life, but when she was 12 years old her speech and language therapist, ruth worked hard and proved all those doctors wrong again the speech and language therapist said that she didn't need speech and language therapy anymore and she's working hard stop physiotherapy for ever. You see all her life she had been proving people wrong, but it was time to prove herself wrong. When ruth decided to be a writer she wanted to write a book, but her subconscious told her otherwise, "you have to be an adult to write and publish a book" but she did her research and learnt that there is NO LIMIT to her dream. So, at the ripe old age of 13 she wrote a book called I feel pink today after her favourite colour PINK anyway this is a bit about the book you're reading.

This is the story of your author (AKA me) Ruth kaputa.

WARNING BEFORE YOU READ THIS BOOK:

Dumb jokes discased as song refences. The author ruth kaputa (ME) is quite a chatter box in the words of my mum. So, if you don't like that YOU CAN LEAVE **(by that I mean close the book and return it) (I was joking please keep reading)**

Season 1- get to know me, (Ruth Kaputa!)

Hi, my name is Ruth kaputa I am currently 13 years old; I'm from London but my mum is from Sierra Leon and my personal assistant I mean dad is from Congo *(my dad is from the south and my mum is from the west of Africa)* and I have 2 brothers one is older Akeem and one younger Nehemiah (but we call him Nehe for short it's nah like a horse). and I love PINK *(not the artist the colour love)* *(although I do like the song "I wanna start a fight")*. My favourite movie is sister act 2 *(back in the habit)* you should really watch it but watch the first sister act to understand the storyline. My favourite actresses are Whoopie Goldberg, Naomi Ackie, Brandy Norwood, and Jennifer Hudson *(if you don't know them you can google them)*. I'm a big music lover. I love glee covers and 90s R&B and pop music like Whitney Houston, Stevie Wonder, Megan Trainor, Adele *(she's not 90s but still)*, and Brandy Norwood and my favourite bands are glee covers, boy 2 men and the cheetah girls. Before I start, I am so sorry If I waffle a lot and the dumb jokes *(wow I talk a lot)*. In this book instead of chapters *(because that sounds boring)* it's going to have seasons like a tv show and instead of me being the author I'm the writer/ executive producer/director. I'm a writer and when I grow up, I want to write storylines for movies and tv shows oh and soaps like neighbours and home and away *(there Australian soaps) (I'm a huge fan of both)*. In this short book we shall talk about different topics from society and Hollywood to self-love and self-esteem, motivation. I have left side cerebral palsy if you don't know what that is then JUST GOOGLE IT *(just joking)* cerebral palsy is a scar in the brain that weakens my muscles on the left side of my body. That's why I use my right hand a lot and I mean a lot in fact as I type this my left arm is a lazy couch potato just sitting there. My wish is as you read this you will treat and see me as a normal person because I am. When I tell people to not call me disabled, they called me differently abled, and I say no because I see myself as normal, I just have challenges that affect my daily life but don't we all. I feel like there must be trust in our relationship between the writer/ executive producer/director and the viewer, so the truth is *(ha-ha see what I did there ruth and truth, no okay)* anyway I'm a three-time published poet I'm telling the truth *(Opps I did it again) (Britney spears)*. in this short book I want teach you how to treat people like me feel normal but anyway, have stories that will make you cry so hard that you laugh and laugh so hard that you cry. I was born on the 1st of April 2010 *(I know 2010 worst year because the spice girls and one direction broke up, I know it was hard, but we powered though the pain)* at 11am *(nearly lunch time so that's why I like food so much) (I know April fools ha-ha)* when I was born the doctors said I had 24 hours to live they basically didn't have faith or hope in me. But *(ha-ha doctors I'm alive)* I was in a coma. So, they had to inject my brain with coffee to wake me up *(even though I don't like coffee)* in fact there's a picture of me in the coma as a baby on the next page and I'm in a wheelchair because I can't walk for long. Now we will be discussing my learning disability. A learning disability is when you don't process things at the same rate as other people, but for me I forget things I have a very good memory, but I forget things academically which affects my learning. Although there are subjects that do somehow stick in my head more than others like history or English but other subjects like maths, science just doesn't stick. It (the learning disability) makes you feel dumb because you know you should know the answers to your test, but you struggle quite a lot. So, this the end of the road *(get it boys 2 men no…ok tough crowd)* any Hoo see you in the next season.

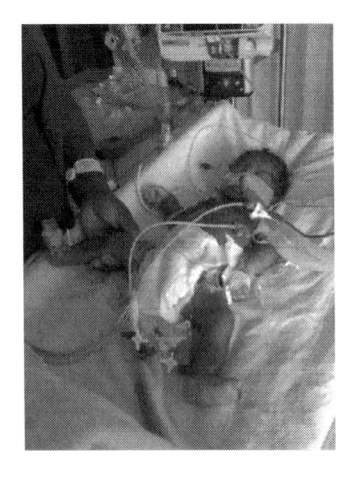

← this is me in the coma (now it looks painful, but I DIDN'T FEEL ANYTHiNG)

season 2 – my poetry

Hi as I said in season 1 I I'm a poet, so I want to show you some of my work. Let's begin!

I know everything – by Ruth Kaputa

Mummy and daddy and are fighting again this time mummy has a BIG SCRACH on her head.

Mummy and daddy are fighting again this time daddy walked out normally he comes back DRUNK but this time he didn't.

Mummy and daddy are fighting again this time mummy came to my room with TEARS DOWN HER FACE as she said "everything is going to be okay" but I knew everything wasn't okay I KNOW EVERYTHING

I know about the ABUSE and the SHARDS OF GLASS mummy picks up every single night.

Normally its mummy and daddy who are fighting its normally daddy SCREAMING at mummy and all Mummy can do is watch the man she once loved turn into An ABUSIVE MONSTER I KNOW EVERYTHING.

I know some of you cried because some of you been though it or you know someone whose been through it, I haven't been through it. I'll give you one more since you're begging.

Dear Gen Z's – by Ruth Kaputa

Dear Gen Z's I'm sorry a million trees have been cut down simply because of logging, agriculture mining and so much more.

Dear Gen Zs as a Gen Z myself I truly thank you on millennials and boomers because as you sat there and watched repeats of George Floyd being brutally murdered by police you decided to say something about it.

I also thank you for learning about how strong black men and woman joined Dr martin Luther king on the Eddison bridge in Alabama to fight for what for what they believed in, and you said it was right.

Dear Gen Z's I'm sorry that America is still called a free country after seeing single mothers choosing nappes over food.

We're not just doing silly TikTok we're doing hashtag black lives matter; we're doing hashtag help stop climate change. We're changing the world so let us. Dear Gen Zs thank you.

Here's one more poem.

Meet my friend – by Ruth Kaputa

Meet my friend p she arrived in a fancy pink limousine with diamonds in a fancy red dress. On the 27th of November 2022 at around 8:30 or 9pm. She burst into my room without knocking. She said, "hi you signed up for the lifetime membership" I said, "I didn't" she said, "every woman is forced to sign up". Only my mum is allowed to see p God forbid my dad or brothers see p we might as well call the church. Some woman sugar quote it as "it's just cramps and bleeding and a lot of chocolate" but to some woman it's a funeral for their womb, the blood Opps mean her red dress reminding them as much as she tries, she will never become a woman unless she has a pram with the sound of a baby crying inside. Meet my friend p when you get to know her you learn that she's not my friend p, she's, my PERIOD.

I hope you liked that it was meant to be a radge poem about periods and about how society views periods because in my work I tell the truth. I personally think that some writers don't tell the truth, they make fairy tales with happy ending's but sometimes that's not always the case.

Now I know this chapter is about my poetry and I know in chapter two I spoke about life and potential. But I would like to share my little theory about life. Do you know how people say that "life is like a roller coaster; it goes up and down" well I think life is abstract. For example, Pablo Picasso one of the greatest artists of all time, when he started his art people thought it was strange but after people realised it was an artistic masterpiece. My point is sometimes life is abstract, going all over the place. but at the end of the day people will realise your life was an artistic masterpiece. I guess that's the end of this season I really hope you enjoyed bye.

season 3- Let me motivate you!

In this season I want to tell you that you can do anything and everybody has potential you just must find it and use it because it took Thomas Edison one thousand times to invent the light bulb, but everyone remembers the one thousandth and one time which was the light bulb he never gave up so maybe it will take you a thousand times to find your potential but never give up because everyone might just remember the a thousandth and first. I have learnt that life is like a house you can kick people out or keep them in. Because you may have negative people that push you down in your life that you need to get rid of and there will be positive people that will push you up. You need to keep the people that are positive. And remember YOU CAN DO ANYTHING YOU SET YOUR HEART AND MIND TOO because you know what they say, "A dream is a wish your heart makes" *(ok maybe it was snow white but it's true)*. Potential can also be what you want to be when you grow up. My journey finding my potential was quite a long road to cross because when I was little, I wanted to be a doctor because I wanted to help people. But then I realized I don't want to work with puck or vomit or pee or poo, but I don't mind blood, oh and medical school is too long, and I believe there's more to life than school *(but school is important)*. Then I wanted to be a pop or gospel singer, but I sound like a frog. Then an actress but I don't have patience for all the rehearsals. And then in year 7 we started doing music tech I liked it, so I wanted to be a music technician but then I realized it was just a hobby. And then I discovered my love for writing through a poetry competition which I won at my school. And here I am a three-time published poet and an author *(well when this gets published)*. So, as you can see from my journey, I had potential it just took me a long time to find my potential. I found it eventually, its ok to take long we are all human. It's okay to make mistakes. I make mistakes, you make mistakes, your mum makes mistakes even your loving grandmother who makes the best cookies make mistakes. And I didn't name it that for no reason so in the table below I will tell you the positives and negatives of why it sucks having a disability, and unfortunately there are more lows than highs, *(in a table)*. Let's begin!

Positives	Negatives
- I can eat in class	- Muscle pain
- I get a one-to-one TA which is a teaching assistant but TAs sound cooler (I call them a personal bestie) - I get to go five minutes early from class. - Proving people wrong when they talk to you like a baby.	- A lot of medication (which taste bad) - People on the street steer at me for being in a wheelchair. - People look at me with pity without getting to know me or my story. - People assuming you can't walk just because you're in a wheelchair.

Now we've been though that your probably confused. On why I can eat in class, you see I have hypoglycaemia which means sometimes the glucose *(sugar)* in my body runs out and if I don't get injected with an injection it has to be in the fridge or there's the gel that I keep that tastes like berries I will collapse or go into a seizer. And I bet your really confused on the last point. Anyway, you need a break from reading me so get your favourite chocolate or if you don't like chocolate stop reading, get out and think about what made you take this book. I was joking because I'm broke aren't we all in this British economy.

season 4 - why loosing people and change can be important.

In other seasons I've already given you advice about life and your potential but in this season, I have else in mind. Lisen, I know this may sound harsh, but its true people will leave you in life and sometimes you think they will be in your life forever, but the truth is people come and go and you think your life won't be the same without them. I had two teachers I was so attached to them, and they told me that they were leaving I was obviously sad because I imagined opening my GCSE results with them there but then I realized that it was their time to leave I also realized that they had an opportunity to better their career. The truth is the world small, they moved away but, in a way, they are around the corner or across the road. So, you have two choices ether stay sad for the rest of your life or stay in touch and be happy for that person or people. So, which one will you choose I'm hoping you choose the second chose. So that's why having to train yourself to deal with change is important in life because things might change but the thing that it changes into might be better. It's okay to cry I cried when they told me they were leaving I cried twice but now I make sure to keep in touch with them. I know this was a short and sad season but as I said before you must deal with change so see you in the next season.

Season 5 - a little more advice for LIFE!

In this season I will give more advice about life. These are the 5 things (in segment's) that we will go through in this season. Before we go through this most of it is about fear *(in billet points)* LET'S BEGIN.

- Have a big imagination in life!
- Jump on idea's you have in life.
- Don't let other people dim your light so they can shine.
- God closes a door to open another one.
- The power of words

Have a big imagination in life!

Now we shall talk about having a big imagination in life and fear limited visions. Fear limited visions are dreams and visions that you have or had that you've never worked on because of fear. It can also be that you can't see yourself being the big and successful person you hope, dream, and want to be. Les brown once said, "fear can crush dreams and kills hope", so when you are afraid you can easily give up your dreams go too. If you let fear control your dreams and hopes, there will be no dreams and hopes. So don't you dare ever let fear control your life and even if your plans don't work in life, you keep trying. For example, if you want to be an actress but your too scared to audition but you read this and you audition, but you didn't get the part you wanted so you don't let fear control you and you audition for a bigger part. So don't ever let fear control you or your life. Another reason is that people can't see themselves with that dream they wanted to accomplish or out of the situation they are in. For example, people in abusive relationships can't or struggle to see themselves without that person. So, what I'm trying to say is that you really should try to see yourself out of the situation and/or accomplishing that dream. See you in the next segment.

Jump on idea's you have in life!

In life if you have ideas that you think it's good then jump on it les brown once said when you die one day and there are three ghosts, those ghosts represent all the idea's that you had but didn't do anything about it and they are upset because the ideas could of made you very successful but you were scared because you thought you would fail in life. I also believe that if you don't take risks in life, it's not life, now I do not mean jump of a cliff in the name of taking risks I just mean jump on those ideas and even if you fail never give up. I have to admit there was a time where I myself did not practise what I have preached, you see when I was around ten or eleven years old this idea of the book came to mind, I thought to do this big project I have to be an adult because of my young age. And the idea was stuck at the back of my head for two to three years. But then I thought "FLIP

IT LIFE IS TOO SHORT to wait". So here I am at home in a pink and white striped very comfy jump suit writing a book. And yes, I do regret not jumping on the idea at the time. But I believe that everything in life happens at a certain time if you make it happen at the time. So, see you in the next segment.

Don't let other people dim your light so they can shine.

I believe that everyone carries a light. And I know we discussed potential but what some people don't know is that other can't handle that light that you carry. So that person will give you reasons to tone it down. For example, if you have the potential to sing. That person might say "you sing too loud" if that happens sing the loudest you can (without destroying your vocal cords of course). Your light belongs to everyone, it'll be illuminated because you were bold enough to let your light shine. Sometimes you walk into a room and your too scared to give 100 percent of your light. Most of the time you think people won't accept 100 percent sometimes they accept 50 or even 20 percent. But hon they only accept little of you because they can't handle your light or their triggered because your light is brighter than the brightest star in the night sky. So please Don't let other people dim your light so they can shine. See you in the next segment.

God closes a door to open another one.

Now before I start, I get that some of you don't believe in God, but this is from my life and my experience. I will tell you a story that happened to me, this story changed my life. This happened 2 or 3 years ago I was choosing where I was going for secondary, and I had my dream school in mind let's call it black coats (because I don't want to get sued). Now the reason I wanted to go to black coats because all my friends were going there and all the club I wanted. I couldn't go because the lift I needed I had to be in year 9 to get the lift. When I didn't get in, I was so sad, (I cried myself to sleep with a bar of chocolate) but I went to another school (the school I am in now) and I made friends and met people who I have truly found inner happiness with who I see every day and those people are the TAs they make my day every day. Then a year later I realized that God close that door to open another door. And I also realized even though I would have had my friends I wouldn't achieve inner happiness. See you in the next segment.

The power of words

Now I believe in the power of words. Words are powerful because they can make you and break you. We use words every single day, sometimes writers like me use big and small words to emphasise how big or how small something is. I believe that words hold more power than anything in the whole world. That's why you should be careful with what words you use every day and think before you say something. You know the phrase "sticks and stones may break your bones, but words will never hurt you", I HATE IT I even made a poem (that's how much I hate the phrase) this is the poem...

sticks and stones may break your bones, but words will never hurt you. Sticks stones breaks bones words never hurt me. You know that used to be motivation in life. But the real reason people say that is to hide the pain its causing inside. Because one, two or even three words can cause you pain. For example, "I love you" because love is like a drug, you go back to the thing that caused you pain in the first place. Love is a drug; people will use you and abuse all in the name of love but you're the one with the choice to let that person or people use you. So, if you want to lose your self-respect just to please other people go ahead and enjoy the ride because no one's stopping you. WORDS HURT!

so please be careful with your words and always use positive words in every situation good or bad, See you in the next season.

Season 6 – why I strongly dislike society.

In this season we are going to discuss why I strongly dislike society. Now in this book we keep it PG so I'm not going to say the H- word *(I think we all know what that is) …. (hate)*. So, these are the reasons I don't like society, *(in bullet points)* LETS BEGIN.

- Racism
- Sexism *(misogyny)*
- Normalising stuff
- Telling you what makes you successful.

- ### Racism

Before we start, I am going to not only target society, but I will also target the film industry and Hollywood, so if you don't like that you can skip this season (don't say I didn't warn you). Let's start with quite sensitive topic, its racism as a black person I just don't get why some people have a problem with other people having melamine. I feel like not only society, but Hollywood and the film industry makes it worse because in nearly every movie or tv show about black people in the south is about drugs, prison, gangs, murder or repainting black people as thugs or criminals. So, what people watch reflex how they treat people in reality. Hollywood and the film industry makes it so realistic, so the racist stereotypical black man thug idea on tv really reflex in the mind of Karen's *(sorry if your name Karen and your nice)*. That's why when I grow up and graduate university, I'm planning to create my own production company called Ruthie's art production. One more thing is those racist women who tell other people and I quote to "go back your country" when they forget that historically the native Americans (modern Indians) were in America first

- ### sexism (misogyny)

Anyway, let's move on to sexism (misogyny) even though we're in the twenty first century mostly men still think of women as objects. In some culture's young the age as me if not younger are still being forced to have babies with men up to double their age whilst others are forced to get marry men double their age. We still have the police who think they have power to sexualise young women to get what they want. And then another reason is us hating on other women/girls over boys because boys will be there forever, I don't get why girls lose 1 hour after school in detention fighting over one boy that's probably not even in school.

- ### Normalising stuff

Now shall discuss society and the film industry normalising stuff this also comes under black people being represented as bad people. Because the industry has normalised the black man thug idea Another thing is that Hollywood normalised in society is that "Africa is a forest" and that "Africa doesn't have water" when in reality Africa is one of the richest continents in the world. It's not just Hollywood I blame for the stereotypical racist Wakanda version of Africa, that they have built in people's mind. I blame the people that chose to believe these racist ideas without doing their research about Africa, I highly recommend you should go you will experience things you never thought you would experience; this is a message for the people think Africa is a country, how do you go through nursery, primary secondary, college and university. Some of you go and get two degrees, master's and PHDs and you still think Africa is a country. In-fact yes Africa is a country, and the capital city is Wakanda (it was a joke). before. Another thing society has normalised is the word "ugly," I believe that no one is born ugly society has just normalised the word to separate people considered less attractive from people considered more attractive, but remember you are so beautiful and never put a price tag on your worth because YOU ARE WORTH THE WORLD AND MORE.

- **Telling you what makes you successful.**

Now before we end the season, I would like to talk about how society telling you what makes you successful. I'll give you three successful people according to society (*in bullet points*).

- Michael Jackson
- Whitney Houston
- Prince

These people were considered very successful until their deaths, all of them did do drugs so they weren't really happy because the media made their lives look good when it wasn't. I believe that success is when you achieve inner happiness. So, these people achieved happiness financially, but they didn't achieve inner happiness. Researchers found out that worldwide only 15% of people are actually engaged in their jobs whilst 85% are unhappy with their jobs, so the 85% of the unhappy people may be making six or even seven figures and the 15% are making less but are still happy. I want to be a writer because when write I go to my own world in my imagination. And I want to be NO I AM THAT 15% of people who have found inner happiness. And if you're that 85% that is unhappy, I need you to take a break and think what makes you happy. Your life is your story, your imagination so you write it. You're the author and with writing you have to take risks so why don't you take risks in life, I'm not saying jump off a cliff or something I mean say you want to be an actor and you have an audition but you don't think you will get the part so you give up but then you decide to take a risk and you audition and you get the lead role, so take risks it might just change your life. So, I guess season 5 was long so see you in season 6.

Season 7 - selflove

in this season I will be teaching you how to love yourself. As people sometimes we get thoughts, thoughts that are not nice, but we are human and its ok. So, these are some positive thoughts that you should think and negative thoughts that you shouldn't think *(in a table)*.

Negative thoughts	Positive thoughts
"I am dumb"	I am so smart
"I am ugly"	My beauty fill's every room I go in
"I am weird"	I am so unique
"no one likes me"	I am so loved
"I wish I could be just like her/him"	I am and will always be myself

Every day I want you to look in the mirror and say the positive thoughts out loud, you can even make a fun poster. Something else you could do is get a picture of a younger version of you put the picture on your mirror so when you are telling yourself those negative thoughts remind yourself that you're calling that little girl or boy "ugly and stupid" *(basically all the negative thoughts)*

Why is selflove so important?

Research shows that having more self- compassion builds resilience in the face of adversity. It means when you practice self-love then you have enough confidence to overcome challenges in life. It is also important because if you don't love yourself, you don't know how to love other people. Self-respect is a fundamental part of self- love because again you will never learn to respect others.

What self-love looks like?

- Forgiving yourself when you mess up.
- Meeting your own needs
- Being assertive
- Not letting others take advantage of or abuse you.
- Prioritizing your health and wellbeing
- Spending time around people who support you and build you up (and avoiding people who don't)

- Asking for help
- Letting go of grudges or anger that holds you back.
- Recognizing your strengths
- Valuing your feelings
- Making healthy choices most of the time
- Living in accordance with your values
- Pursuing your interests and goals
- Challenging yourself
- Holding yourself accountable
- Giving yourself healthy treats
- Accepting your imperfections
- Setting realistic expectations

Some self- love quotes you can use.

Now I have gave you positive thoughts you can think and practise these are some quotes you can use and decorate your room with *(in bullet points) (whoop, whoop)*.

- If you have the ability to love, love yourself first." – Charles Bukowski
- "The man who does not value himself, cannot value anything or anyone." – Ayn Rand
- "Be the love you never received." – Rune Lazuli
- "Love yourself first and everything else falls into line." – Lucille Ball
- "Talk to yourself like someone you love." – Brene Brown
- "To fall in love with yourself is the first secret to happiness." – Robert Morely
- "No one can make you feel inferior without your consent." – Eleanor Roosevelt
- "You are free, you are powerful, you are good, you are love, you have value, you have a purpose." – Unknown
- "You carry so much love in your heart. Give some to yourself." —R.Z.
- "How you love yourself is how you teach others to love you." —Rupi Kaur
- "Make yourself a priority." —Unknown

Fun facts about self- love

Now we've talked about why self -love is important, what it looks like, and we have looked at expert quotes and now we shall look at fun facts before end the seasons.

- Accepting yourself can make you happier.
- It could encourage you to reach those health goals.
- Self-compassion may help with mental health issues.

- It can push you to stop procrastinating.
- Loving yourself can lead you through adversity.
- If you don't love yourself, you will regret it later in life.

Well, I guess this shall be the end of the season, just a disclaimer season 6 and 7 both have to do with self-confidence. See you in the next season.

Season 8- Self esteem

In this season, in the topic of last season *(self- love)* we will be discussing self- esteem. So hopefully the things I told you about positive and negative thoughts and self- love worked and built up your self- esteem.

What is self- esteem?

Self-esteem is how we value and perceive ourselves. It's based on our opinions and beliefs about ourselves, which can feel difficult to change. We might also think of this as self-confidence. Its okay if your self-esteem low because we are human all that matters is that you fix it with these tips.

Your self-esteem can affect whether you:

- Like and value yourself as a person!
- Can make decisions and assert yourself.
- Recognise your strengths!
- Feel able to try new or difficult things.
- Show kindness towards yourself.
- Move past mistakes without blaming yourself unfairly.
- Take the time you need for yourself.
- Believe you matter and are good enough!
- Believe you deserve happiness!

How to improve your self esteem

- Be kind to yourself.
- Try to recognise the positives.
- Build a good support network.
- Try taking therapy.
- Set yourself a challenge.
- Look after yourself.

Now let's through why you should use these 6 reasons.

Be kind to yourself.

- **Get to know yourself.** For example, what makes you happy and what you value in life. You might find it helpful to write this in a journal.
- **Try to challenge unkind thoughts about yourself.** You might automatically put yourself down. If you find yourself doing this, it can help to ask: "Would I talk to a friend in this way?"

- **Say positive things to yourself.** Some people like to do this in front of a mirror. It can feel strange at first, but you may feel more comfortable the more you do it.
- **Practise saying no.** Being assertive can be difficult if you're not used to it. But agreeing to too many things to please others can draining. It could help to pause, take a breath, and think about how you feel before agreeing to do something you don't want to.
- **Try to avoid comparing yourself to others.** For example, it might help to limit how much time you spend on social media or online communities. What other people often choose to share about their lives isn't always the full picture.
- **Do something nice for yourself.** For example, making your favourite meal or playing a game you enjoy.

Try to recognise the positives!

- **Celebrate your successes.** No matter how small they may seem, take time to praise yourself. For example, this could be getting outside for a walk or doing some tidying.
- **Accept compliments.** You could save them up to look over when you're feeling low or doubting yourself.
- **Ask people what they like about you** if you feel comfortable. They may recognise things that you don't think about yourself.
- **Write a list of things you like about yourself.** For example, this could be a skill that you've learnt, or something you do to help other people.

Build a good support network.

- **Talk to someone you trust.** Having someone listen to you and show they care can help. If you aren't able to open up to someone close to you, you could call a helpline to speak to someone anonymously.
- **Focus on positive relationships.** It might feel difficult to control who you spend time with. But where possible, it can help to spend more time with people who make you feel good about yourself.
- **Try peer support.** Making connections with people who have similar or shared experiences can help.

Try taking therapy.

Talking therapies can help with building self-esteem. They can also help you find ways to cope with experiences that affect how you feel about yourself.

set yourself a challenge!

- Try volunteering. You might decide to volunteer your time for something you feel passionate about. For more information on volunteering, see the Volunteer by Do-IT website.
- Set small goals. This could help things feel more manageable and give you a greater sense of achievement.
- Learn something new. For example, this could be trying a new hobby or creative activity. Or taking time to read a book about a new subject.

Look after yourself!

- Try to get enough sleep. Getting too little or too much sleep can have a negative impact on how you feel. See our pages on coping with sleep problems for more information.
- Think about your diet. Eating regularly and keeping your blood sugar stable can make a difference to your mood and energy levels. See our pages on food and mood for more information.
- Try to do some physical activity. Being active can help your mental wellbeing. This may include helping to improve your self-esteem. See our pages on physical activity for more information.
- Spend time outside. Being in green space can often help how you feel. See our pages on nature and mental health for more information.

- Practise mindfulness and meditation. For example, you could try Headspace's meditation course for self-esteem.
- Try to avoid recreational drugs and alcohol. You might want to use recreational drugs or alcohol to cope with difficult feelings about yourself. But in the long run they can make you feel worse and can prevent you from dealing with underlying problems. See our pages on recreational drugs and alcohol for more information.
- Sign up to a self-help programme. For example, you could try our supported self-help programme if you are in Wales. Or you could use the Reading Well books scheme to find books to help with your self-esteem.

Try doing these things and you never know maybe it will change your life. The positive thoughts from season 6 isn't only self-love but it could boost your self-esteem. For some people self-esteem is little voice in their head that says, "your rubbish, your fat, what's the point, you're not cut out for this" and so on.

What can cause low self-esteem?

The things that affect our self-esteem are different for everyone. Your self-esteem might change suddenly. Or you might have had low self-esteem for a while.

There are lots of things in life that may contribute to low self-esteem.

- Being bullied or abused
- experiencing prejudice, discrimination or stigma, including racism
- Losing your job or difficulty finding employment
- Problems at work or while studying
- Physical health problems
- Relationship problems, separation, or divorce
- Problems with money or housing
- Worries about your appearance and body image.
- feeling pressure to meet unrealistic expectations, for example through social media.

Is low self-esteem a mental health problem?

Low self-esteem isn't a mental health problem in itself. But mental health and self-esteem can be closely linked.

Some of the signs of low self-esteem can be signs of mental health problem. This is especially if they last for a long time or affect your daily life. For example:

- feeling hopeless or worthless
- blaming yourself unfairly
- hating yourself
- worrying about unable to do things.

Having a mental health problem could also cause you to have low self-esteem. And it might feel harder to cope or take steps to improve your self-esteem if you struggle with your mental health. Having a mental health problem could also cause you to have low self-esteem. And it might feel harder to cope or take steps to improve your self-esteem if you struggle with your mental health.

Thank you to mind the company that helps people with their mental health that I got some of this information from.

Season 9 – jokes and funny stories

In this season I will tell you jokes and funny stories (because face it, it's been a little bit depressing)

Joke1#

There's a man named bob. Bob doesn't have any arms. Knock knock who's there it isn't bob. (I'm sorry if that offended anyone without arms)

Joke2#

(we're with our friend bob again) bob died and when he arrived in heaven God took him to a huge room full of clock on the walls some were ticking fast others slow, God says each clock you see on the see represent all countries of the world, the faster the clocks tick the more sins that country commits daily and the slower the clocks the less sins a country commits daily. So, bob says "where's America's clock" (because he was from America) (well when he was alive) so God sighs and says unfortunately, America has been turned into a ceiling fan.

Joke 3#

Once I was on my way to school singing, I'm still standing (the glee cover) when I realised, I'm in a wheelchair. (I'm sorry if that offended anyone in a wheelchair).

1st funny story

In this story me and my family had a fire drill in my house one afternoon and we were going down, we were in the house and the guess what my dad did instead of walking down he got a piece of fried chicken. I like fried chicken is way too greasy, why not just take a chocolate bar or something.

2nd funny story

I was on the bus in the wheelchair, there was this girl and her mother she was staring at me so do you know what I did, I stuck my tongue at her. Now you must be thinking "ruth that wasn't nice" but honestly it makes me feel abnormal. And abnormal doesn't feel nice.

3rd funny story

This other story happened when I was in the bus *(again)* to a hospital appointment *there* was a lady sitting next to my mum then she says that I should go to a catholic church to get healing and deliverance. You see my mum is overprotective, so she started screaming at the lady. Don't worry there one more story, there was this lady and her dog, and her dog started barking at me and guess what she said. She said, "sorry my dog is afraid of wheelchairs" I can't even tell you how stupid that sounds, I was like "hon/babes/Babs I think we're all afraid of dogs calm down".

4th funny story

(this story did not happen on a bus thank God) me and my mum was watching my 1000-pound life (it's a show about overweight people and the way they live their lives and the struggles they go through being overweight). Anyway, my mum turns to me and says "we should eat healthier" so I went to the dining table and got a plan donut (because my mum made donut the day before she made donuts because she's a baker) and I put that bad boy in the microwave for 20 seconds put some Nutella on that bad boy and ate it right in front of her.

5th funny story

As I mentioned in season 1, I have a brother who is 9-year-old currently and if you have a younger brother/ sibling you would know sometimes they can say/ do things that are really dumb for no reason at all. One time my mum told him to turn off the stove/cooker then he went to the kitchen and then he came back, looked at me and my mum with a died straight face and said what's a stove. My mum was doing my hair at the time, but I fell on the floor laughing,

6th funny story

Before I start this story, I have to give you a bit of background information I get laughing fits and sometimes I just think of funny things and the laughing fits just come out, but I have learnt to control them over the years. So I was in English class, we were writing a paragraph about Beowulf, so I decided to make mine funny, so I made a joke in my paragraph. So, when my teacher was asking us who wants to up at the front of the class to share, I went up and then when I got up to the part when the joke pops up and the laughing fit came out. I couldn't control it, so the teacher just said "lets just give ruth a break" at the time it was embarrassing but now I laugh about it.

Season 10 – farewell season

Unfortunately, but fortunately for the haters this is the last season of this book but before we end, I would love to say thank you to the people in my life who has supported this journey. **(and in different fonts eeeee I love fonts)**

1st I would love to thank God for putting the idea in head to write this book and for the art of writing.

2nd I would love to thank my parents (mostly my mum because didn't tell him as a surprise) for not letting me give up on my dreams.

3rd I would love to thank my two brothers for always being there for me.

4th I would love to thank extended family for supporting my ongoing writing career.

5th I would love to thank my pastor divine for everything he has done for me.

I would like to thank my good friend D for making me laugh each time I see him.

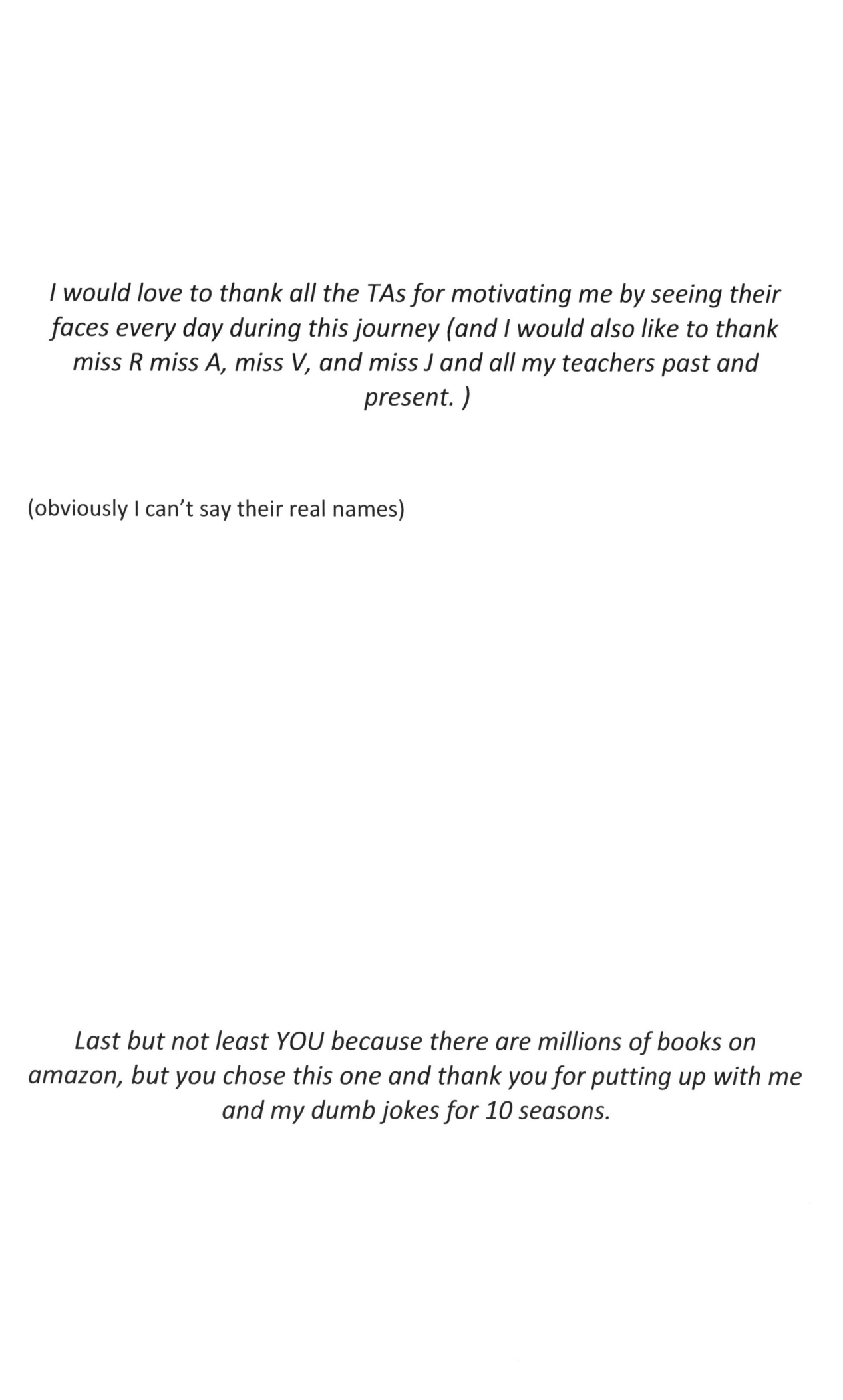

I would love to thank all the TAs for motivating me by seeing their faces every day during this journey (and I would also like to thank miss R miss A, miss V, and miss J and all my teachers past and present.)

(obviously I can't say their real names)

Last but not least YOU because there are millions of books on amazon, but you chose this one and thank you for putting up with me and my dumb jokes for 10 seasons.

If you thought this is the end of me, you are definitely wrong. Its NEVER the end of ruth kaputa (I mean the end of the book not me) that was one more very dumb joke for the road.

Anyway, I need chocolate now.

Bye gorgeous.

Printed in Great Britain
by Amazon

- **Say positive things to yourself.** Some people like to do this in front of a mirror. It can feel strange at first, but you may feel more comfortable the more you do it.
- **Practise saying no.** Being assertive can be difficult if you're not used to it. But agreeing to too many things to please others can draining. It could help to pause, take a breath, and think about how you feel before agreeing to do something you don't want to.
- **Try to avoid comparing yourself to others.** For example, it might help to limit how much time you spend on social media or online communities. What other people often choose to share about their lives isn't always the full picture.
- **Do something nice for yourself.** For example, making your favourite meal or playing a game you enjoy.

Try to recognise the positives!

- **Celebrate your successes**. No matter how small they may seem, take time to praise yourself. For example, this could be getting outside for a walk or doing some tidying.
- **Accept compliments**. You could save them up to look over when you're feeling low or doubting yourself.
- **Ask people what they like about you** if you feel comfortable. They may recognise things that you don't think about yourself.
- **Write a list of things you like about yourself.** For example, this could be a skill that you've learnt, or something you do to help other people.

Build a good support network.

- **Talk to someone you trust**. Having someone listen to you and show they care can help. If you aren't able to open up to someone close to you, you could call a helpline to speak to someone anonymously.
- **Focus on positive relationships.** It might feel difficult to control who you spend time with. But where possible, it can help to spend more time with people who make you feel good about yourself.
- **Try peer support.** Making connections with people who have similar or shared experiences can help.

Try taking therapy.

Talking therapies can help with building self-esteem. They can also help you find ways to cope with experiences that affect how you feel about yourself.

set yourself a challenge!

- Try volunteering. You might decide to volunteer your time for something you feel passionate about. For more information on volunteering, see the Volunteer by Do-IT website.
- Set small goals. This could help things feel more manageable and give you a greater sense of achievement.
- Learn something new. For example, this could be trying a new hobby or creative activity. Or taking time to read a book about a new subject.

Look after yourself!

- Try to get enough sleep. Getting too little or too much sleep can have a negative impact on how you feel. See our pages on coping with sleep problems for more information.
- Think about your diet. Eating regularly and keeping your blood sugar stable can make a difference to your mood and energy levels. See our pages on food and mood for more information.
- Try to do some physical activity. Being active can help your mental wellbeing. This may include helping to improve your self-esteem. See our pages on physical activity for more information.
- Spend time outside. Being in green space can often help how you feel. See our pages on nature and mental health for more information.

- Practise mindfulness and meditation. For example, you could try Headspace's meditation course for self-esteem.
- Try to avoid recreational drugs and alcohol. You might want to use recreational drugs or alcohol to cope with difficult feelings about yourself. But in the long run they can make you feel worse and can prevent you from dealing with underlying problems. See our pages on recreational drugs and alcohol for more information.
- Sign up to a self-help programme. For example, you could try our supported self-help programme if you are in Wales. Or you could use the Reading Well books scheme to find books to help with your self-esteem.

Try doing these things and you never know maybe it will change your life. The positive thoughts from season 6 isn't only self-love but it could boost your self-esteem. For some people self-esteem is little voice in their head that says, "your rubbish, your fat, what's the point, you're not cut out for this" and so on.

What can cause low self-esteem?

The things that affect our self-esteem are different for everyone. Your self-esteem might change suddenly. Or you might have had low self-esteem for a while.

There are lots of things in life that may contribute to low self-esteem.

- Being bullied or abused
- experiencing prejudice, discrimination or stigma, including racism
- Losing your job or difficulty finding employment
- Problems at work or while studying
- Physical health problems
- Relationship problems, separation, or divorce
- Problems with money or housing
- Worries about your appearance and body image.
- feeling pressure to meet unrealistic expectations, for example through social media.

Is low self-esteem a mental health problem?

Low self-esteem isn't a mental health problem in itself. But mental health and self-esteem can be closely linked.

Some of the signs of low self-esteem can be signs of mental health problem. This is especially if they last for a long time or affect your daily life. For example:

- feeling hopeless or worthless
- blaming yourself unfairly
- hating yourself
- worrying about unable to do things.

Having a mental health problem could also cause you to have low self-esteem. And it might feel harder to cope or take steps to improve your self-esteem if you struggle with your mental health. Having a mental health problem could also cause you to have low self-esteem. And it might feel harder to cope or take steps to improve your self-esteem if you struggle with your mental health.

Thank you to mind the company that helps people with their mental health that I got some of this information from.

Season 9 – jokes and funny stories

In this season I will tell you jokes and funny stories (because face it, it's been a little bit depressing)

Joke1#

There's a man named bob. Bob doesn't have any arms. Knock knock who's there it isn't bob. (I'm sorry if that offended anyone without arms)

Joke2#

(we're with our friend bob again) bob died and when he arrived in heaven God took him to a huge room full of clock on the walls some were ticking fast others slow, God says each clock you see on the see represent all countries of the world, the faster the clocks tick the more sins that country commits daily and the slower the clocks the less sins a country commits daily. So, bob says "where's America's clock" (because he was from America) (well when he was alive) so God sighs and says unfortunately, America has been turned into a ceiling fan.

Joke 3#

Once I was on my way to school singing, I'm still standing (the glee cover) when I realised, I'm in a wheelchair. (I'm sorry if that offended anyone in a wheelchair).

1st funny story

In this story me and my family had a fire drill in my house one afternoon and we were going down, we were in the house and the guess what my dad did instead of walking down he got a piece of fried chicken. I like fried chicken is way too greasy, why not just take a chocolate bar or something.

2nd funny story

I was on the bus in the wheelchair, there was this girl and her mother she was staring at me so do you know what I did, I stuck my tongue at her. Now you must be thinking "ruth that wasn't nice" but honestly it makes me feel abnormal. And abnormal doesn't feel nice.

3rd funny story

This other story happened when I was in the bus *(again)* to a hospital appointment *there* was a lady sitting next to my mum then she says that I should go to a catholic church to get healing and deliverance. You see my mum is overprotective, so she started screaming at the lady. Don't worry there one more story, there was this lady and her dog, and her dog started barking at me and guess what she said. She said, "sorry my dog is afraid of wheelchairs" I can't even tell you how stupid that sounds, I was like "hon/babes/Babs I think we're all afraid of dogs calm down".

4th funny story

(this story did not happen on a bus thank God) me and my mum was watching my 1000-pound life (it's a show about overweight people and the way they live their lives and the struggles they go through being overweight). Anyway, my mum turns to me and says "we should eat healthier" so I went to the dining table and got a plan donut (because my mum made donut the day before she made donuts because she's a baker) and I put that bad boy in the microwave for 20 seconds put some Nutella on that bad boy and ate it right in front of her.

5th funny story

As I mentioned in season 1, I have a brother who is 9-year-old currently and if you have a younger brother/ sibling you would know sometimes they can say/ do things that are really dumb for no reason at all. One time my mum told him to turn off the stove/cooker then he went to the kitchen and then he came back, looked at me and my mum with a died straight face and said what's a stove. My mum was doing my hair at the time, but I fell on the floor laughing,

6th funny story

Before I start this story, I have to give you a bit of background information I get laughing fits and sometimes I just think of funny things and the laughing fits just come out, but I have learnt to control them over the years. So I was in English class, we were writing a paragraph about Beowulf, so I decided to make mine funny, so I made a joke in my paragraph. So, when my teacher was asking us who wants to up at the front of the class to share, I went up and then when I got up to the part when the joke pops up and the laughing fit came out. I couldn't control it, so the teacher just said "lets just give ruth a break" at the time it was embarrassing but now I laugh about it.

Season 10 – farewell season

Unfortunately, but fortunately for the haters this is the last season of this book but before we end, I would love to say thank you to the people in my life who has supported this journey. ***(and in different fonts eeeee I love fonts)***

1st I would love to thank God for putting the idea in head to write this book and for the art of writing.

2nd I would love to thank my parents (mostly my mum because didn't tell him as a surprise) for not letting me give up on my dreams.

3rd I would love to thank my two brothers for always being there for me.

4th I would love to thank extended family for supporting my ongoing writing career.

5th I would love to thank my pastor divine for everything he has done for me.

I would like to thank my good friend D for making me laugh each time I see him.

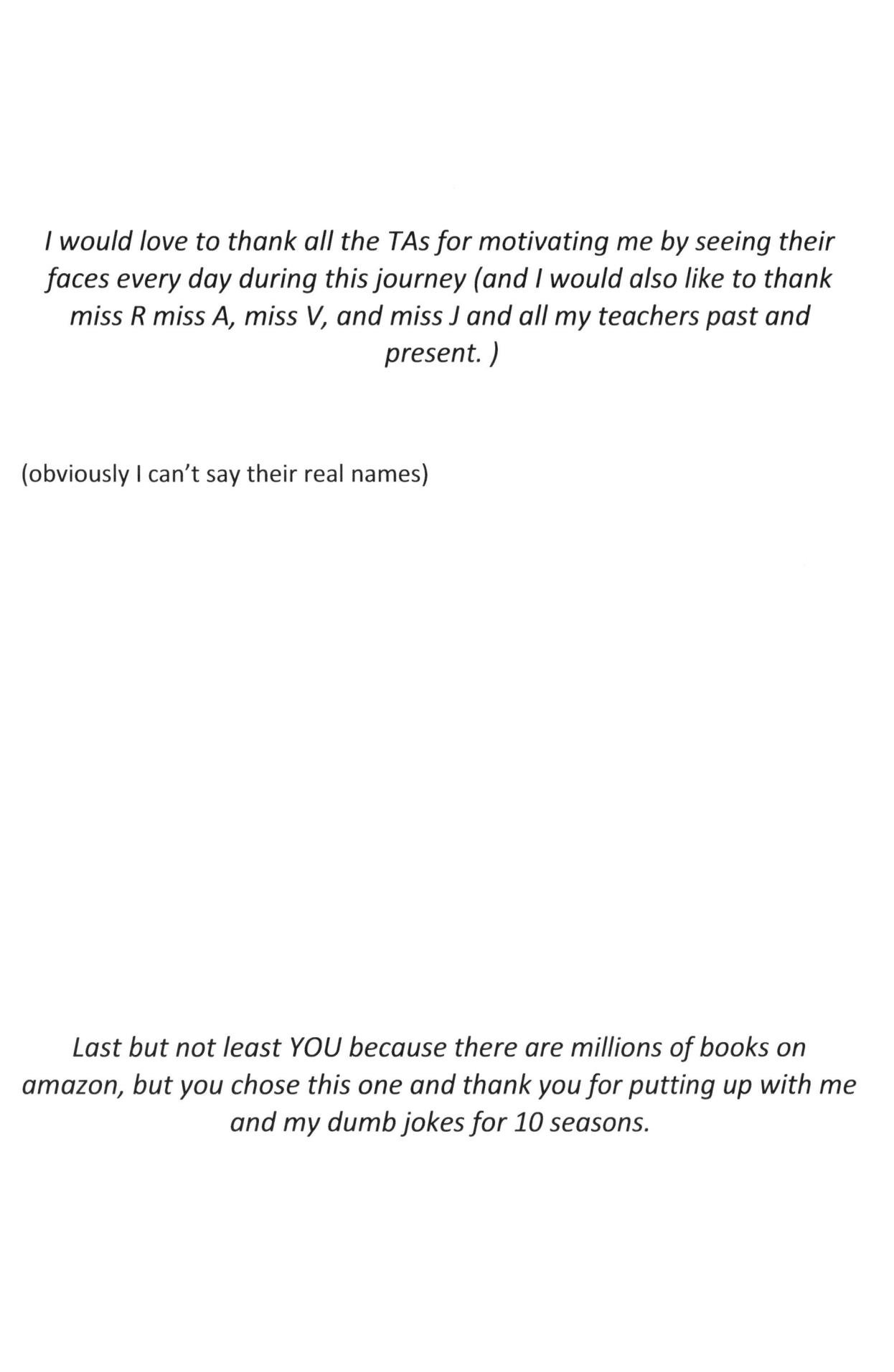

I would love to thank all the TAs for motivating me by seeing their faces every day during this journey (and I would also like to thank miss R miss A, miss V, and miss J and all my teachers past and present.)

(obviously I can't say their real names)

Last but not least YOU because there are millions of books on amazon, but you chose this one and thank you for putting up with me and my dumb jokes for 10 seasons.

If you thought this is the end of me, you are definitely wrong. Its NEVER the end of ruth kaputa (I mean the end of the book not me) that was one more very dumb joke for the road.

Anyway, I need chocolate now.

Bye gorgeous.

Printed in Great Britain
by Amazon